THE BEAUTY OF
CATS

THE BEAUTY OF
CATS

EDITED BY CHARLENE TUTTLE ADAMS
PHOTOGRAPHY BY ROBERT & EUNICE PEARCY

JG
PRESS

Published in the USA 1995 by JG Press
Distributed by World Publications, Inc.

The JG Press imprint is a trademark of JG Press, Inc.
455 Somerset Avenue
North Dighton, MA 02764

Produced by
Brompton Books Corporation
15 Sherwood Place
Greenwich, Connecticut 06830

ISBN 1-57215-086-6

Printed in China

Edited and captioned by Bill Yenne
Designed by Ruth DeJauregui

Page 1: A beautiful black and white shorthair pauses
from playing with string to pose warily on her pillow.
Page 2: A young Somali enjoys a romp amid the efflu-
via of Christmas afternoon.
Below: A kitten on the keys? No, just a proud Persian
at rest.

Photo Credits:
All photographs copyright © Robert and Eunice
Pearcy.

CONTENTS

INTRODUCTION

Below: This beautiful golden queen rests on her pad at the card shop. It's daytime and she's off duty. After closing time, however, she will become a huntress.
Opposite: Beautiful Blue Eyes, a kitten with a spinning wheel.

Despite their well-founded reputation for aloofness, cats are wonderful and loving pets. As author and cat lover Ann Fadiman has pointed out, owning a dog is a utilitarian pleasure, but owning a cat is an aesthetic joy. As she puts it so succinctly, cats are poetry. Cats have, in fact, been an important part of the world's mythology.

The cat has long been a companion of man. In the days of old the cat caught mice and other vermin, protecting the granaries of the farmer. During the Middle Ages, despite superstition and its bad reputation, having a cat meant the family might survive the dreaded Black Death. Today people spend long, stressful hours on the job and come home to the relaxing therapy of their purring cats. Unlike dogs, most cats are happy apartment dwellers, content to sit on a window sill and soak up the sun's rays all day, and then join their owners for dinner and perhaps a little late night television. Popular talk show host Jay Leno and his tabby Cheesler like to watch television together. Cheesler loves to

watch wildlife films with birds and creatures that she can hunt. Jay has noticed that she doesn't care for programs on elephants.

As any cat owner knows, the relationship between cat and owner is as nearly perfect as such a relationship can be. Our cat's place in our scheme of life is secure. Our cat's actions and well-being have an important bearing on many phases of our daily affairs. To most of us the cat appeals directly to our better nature. The cat has an almost universal appeal to members of the human family, regardless of location, age, or occupation.

The cat occupies an important place in our lives and is deserving of proportionate consideration. As an intelligent animal it is not merely a creature of reflexes and instincts. Cats are an important part of not only our lives, but our culture, as they have been for centuries. We know, for instance, of the prominence of the cat to the ancient Egyptians. We can see by the evidence that remains that cats were once a revered part of Egyptian life.

Cats have a remarkable ability to sense human emotions and are often used in therapy. Somehow, a purring cat can break through the mental barriers that humans use to guard their emotions. In prisons, the most hardened criminals will adopt wild kittens and tame them. Caring for a cat can release tension and relieve loneliness and feelings of isolation.

Laughter really is the best medicine, not only for the young and healthy, but also for the elderly. The games and antics of a cat keeps both its owner and itself amused. Cats do indeed make wonderful companions for older people. Comedian George Burns and his Persian named Willie, his favorite companion into his 90s, have a good rapport. 'She laughs at all the right spots,' Burns chuckled.

Below: A healthy, but sleepy, tom rests amid his owner's rag dolls.
Opposite: This grey beauty is distinctively marked. The cat is an object of beauty and a joy to behold.
Overleaf: What can be more engaging than a kitten but a quartet of kittens?

PEOPLE AND OUR CATS

Below: The Persians are among the more popular of longhaired breeds.
Opposite: Abyssinians, with their golden eyes and coats, are descended from cats imported from East Africa in the nineteenth century.

What was the origin of the cat? Charles Darwin said that he had never been able to determine whether domestic cats were descended from several distinct species or had only been modified by occasional crosses. History records many varieties: the African and Egyptian cats; the Asiatic cats, including the Persians, the Angoras and the Siamese; and finally the European cats, now known as the Domestic Shorthairs and the Norwegian Forest Cat.

The Egyptians were among the first great civilizations to deify their domestic cats, although the origin of Egypt's sacred cats is unknown. They may have been tamed Kaffir cats, a species of feline native to Asia and Africa. Of the modern breeds of cats, the Abyssinian appears to be the direct descendant of the Egyptian cats.

The statues of the goddess Bast (also known as Pasht), showing her with a cat head or with cats at her feet, the statues brought from Thebes and Bubastis and now in Cairo,

the British Museum in London, the Metropolitan Museum of Art in New York and numerous other museums throughout the world, tell a story that cannot be denied. So too do the many cat cemeteries that have been uncovered in Egypt, with the small feline mummies in their cases, rich with inlay work of gold and gems and wrought with carvings representing food that was to sustain the cat in its journey through eternity.

Like most of the ancient peoples, the Egyptians used beasts and birds, as well as humans, to symbolize their gods, but the cat preeminently expressed their conception that good and evil exist side by side, that light is born of darkness and day follows night. Cats were not only the attendants of Bast, the beneficent and kindly, but of Sekhmet, the goddess of war. Perhaps that was because of the many-sided nature of the cat. We have often seen one of our own cats purring, an affectionate pet, quickly transformed by the appearance of an alien feline into a shrieking warrior defending his territory. Feline nature has not changed since the days of the Pharaohs.

Because cats have excellent night vision, Bast was occasionally pictured as the cat-moon, holding the sun in her eye at night. One can imagine that the first Egyptian philosopher, looking into his cat's phosphorescent eyes at night, saw a reflection and interpreted it as a promise that the sun would surely return. But the worship of the cat began before the dawn of history and we have no record of its beginnings.

On an island in the Nile in Lower Egypt, north of Bilbeis, where the city of Bubastis lay, travellers may see the remains of the temple once dedicated to Bast as the protector of cats. Herodotus left a description of it in its glory: a building of the finest red granite, five hundred feet long, standing in a spacious enclosure in which were tree-shaded canals and lakes. The vestibule was lined with statues six cubits high, and in the innermost shrine was the most sacred figure of Bast.

Also at Bubastis was the necropolis where cats who died in that vicinity were interred. Herodotus said that some Egyptians who lived far from the temple would send their

Below and opposite:
Today's Egyptian Mau is similar to the cats immortalized in the art of Ancient Egypt. Cats were highly regarded by the Pharaohs and enjoyed a place of importance in court life.

revered pets to be buried there, believing they would rest better in the abode of their patroness. But there were also cat cemeteries in other towns where Bast was worshiped. One was discovered in the grottoes at Beni Hasan, with hundreds of thousands of cat mummies arranged on shelves. If the Egyptians had known what the irreverent Europeans would do with the small bodies so carefully placed there, they would have buried them deeper. The little mummies were shipped (except the few that were sold to tourists) to Liverpool to be sold at auction and used as fertilizer for English crops.

The mummy cases preserved in museums are of extraordinary variety and beauty. Some are made of linen, with palm-leaf ears and disks to represent eyes, and some of wood or bronze or clay, either shaped as a coffin or made in a cat's form, with eyes of crystal,

Below: The Egyptians created statues of their cats. This cat, who obviously had an Egyptian Mau grandparent, strikes a statuesque pose.
Opposite: *The Abyssinian was bred for its striking similarity to a lioness.*

gold and black obsidian. There are also cat amulets that the Egyptians wore, and in the British Museum is one quaint wooden cat with a movable jaw, perhaps a toy that a little child played with on the banks of the Nile.

Those ancient Egyptians, believing that death was only a temporary suspension of life which would be renewed if the body was preserved, went to every effort to give their cats a chance of resurrection. Centuries later, when they decided that there was a Paradise — a glorified Egypt where cats and people might live and hunt in sunlit fields forever — they provided for the little cat souls by assigning a goddess to guide and protect them on their journey.

Above the heaven for commoners was the one where the Pharaohs lived with their favorite cats. Cats, like people, were graded in rank, dignities and honors. Even in Paradise some cats played in the fields while others sat quietly with their royal masters in a glorious eternity.

Egyptian cats were revered for their fertility. The sistrum, an Egyptian musical instru-

ment used in religious ceremonies, was designed to represent the principle of life. It always had the figure of a cat on its apex as the emblem of eternal fruitfulness. Cats also represented strength in the war of good against evil and darkness.

When the god Ra, who personified the life-giving sun, battled the malevolent serpent Rerek, he took the form of a cat. It was believed that, in the terrible wars that raged in the skies during solar eclipses, it was the celestial cat who leaped on the serpent and slew him.

Though the Bible makes no mention of felines, cats *are* mentioned in the Talmud. The Talmudic name for cat is 'the pouncer,' and there are references to its mousing habits and its attachment to the home it has chosen.

In his book *The Gospel of the Holy Twelve*, Reverend GJ Ouseley speaks of the birth of Christ, saying: 'There were in the same cave an ox and a horse and an ass, and a sheep, and beneath the manger a cat with her little ones, and there were doves also, overhead, and each had its mate.'

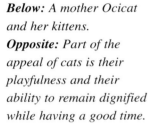

Below: A mother Ocicat and her kittens.
Opposite: Part of the appeal of cats is their playfulness and their ability to remain dignified while having a good time.

HC **Brooke**, an English cat-lover and an early editor of the *Cat Gossip Magazine*, wrote this amusing poem dedicated to an Abyssinian cat:

When The Nile Was Young

'Fore thee a priesthood, wise in ancient
   lore,
Spread offerings rich and rare.
And when thy time upon this Earth was
   o'er
Then, jewel-decked, thou shards't the
   Pharaoh's tomb.
O Bast, look downward through the
   centuries
And see thy children.
Timorous through the streets
Some crouch, the sport of every ruffian
   lad:
Cold-blooded torturers wrench their
   tender limbs
In name of science.
Yet scarce a soul lifts a protesting voice.
We are not pagans, as those sons of Nile!

Cats like silence, order and quietness, and no place is so proper for them as the study of a man of letters.

Whether cats are really interested in the business of writing, or only pretend to be, is unknown, but the effect is the same. They are so tactful about it, so restful and soothing. They sit quietly on the desk or gaze intently at the writer's tapping fingers. They do like to sleep on the keyboard and it is a little inconvenient but, with a bit of urging, they will gracefully retire.

How fortunate are cats such as Calvin, who Charles Dudley Warner writes of with such understanding in *My Summer in a Garden*.

'Writing always interested him,' Charles Warner said. 'Until he understood it he wanted to hold the pen. But he was never obtrusive. He would sit quietly in my study for hours, then moved by a delicate affection, come and pull at my sleeve until he could touch my face with his nose and then go away contented. He could do almost everything but speak, and you would declare sometimes that you could see a pathetic longing to do that in his intelligent face.'

Calvin must have craved literary surroundings. He walked one day 'out of the great unknown' into the house of Harriet Beecher Stowe. 'It was as if he had inquired at the door if this was her home, and, upon being assured that it was, had decided to dwell there.'

When the famous author moved to her winter home in Florida, Calvin went to live with the Warners. He divided his time between the garden, the study and the drawing room when there were guests. He did not care for the kitchen except at dinnertime.

When Calvin died, 'A little shock went through the neighborhood and his friends, one after another, came to see him.' His burial was simple, because the Warners felt that any parade or sentimental nonsense would be distasteful to him.

'He was always a mystery,' the biography ends. 'I did not know whence he came, I do not know whither he has gone. I would not weave one spray of falsehood in the wreath I

Below: The huntress relaxes, but not without keeping a wary eye out for butterflies that must be challenged.
Opposite: Kittens always bring joy to a home.

lay upon his grave.' French writers are particularly fond of cats. Gautier had a house full of cats until the siege of Paris in 1870 decimated them. Best of all he loved Gavroche, a charitable creature who would 'bring in from the streets gaunt and ragged cats, who devoured in a scurry of fright the food laid aside for him.'

Victor Hugo, Prosper Merimee and Anatole France all had their favorite cats. Cardinal Richelieu found diversion in his. Montaigne wrote, 'When I play with my cat who knows whether she amuses herself with me or I with her?'

Pierre Loti left charming accounts of his cats, Moumoutte Blanche and Moumoutte Chinoise, but he could sympathize with less fortunate ones too. There are few things more poignant that his story of the lonely, old, sick cat to whom he gave what he believed was merciful death. But from the brink the cat's eyes followed him:

'Why were you in such a hurry for me to meet my fate? If it had not been for you I would have been able to drag out life a little longer, to have still had certain little thoughts, cares, fancies of my own. I had still strength enough left to spring to the sills of the windows, where the dogs would not trouble me too much. In the morning, when the sun shone there, I could have looked about me and seen life. Instead of which I am about to be dissolved into I know not what. I will be no more.'

It was the waifs and strays of catdom that Samuel Butler, seventeenth century English poet, loved to take in and save if he could. George Moore, master of beautiful prose, liked plain, shorthaired cats of plebeian origin. Thomas Hardy, on the other hand, had a Persian to keep him company. Henry James sometimes wrote with a cat on his shoulder and Walter Pater always had them about.

Cats were an acquired taste for Walter Scott. In early life he disliked them, but then he met Hinse of Hinsefield, and Hinse came to live with him and taught him many things. 'Cats are a mysterious kind of folk,' he wrote. 'There is more passing in their minds than we are aware of.'

Samuel Johnson, though, knew what was passing in the mind of his cat Hodge when Hodge wanted oysters. Hodge left him in no doubt, and there are few pictures more lovable than that of the gruff old doctor laying down his pen and stomping out to buy Hodge's favorite food.

Below and opposite: A selection of images of mixed breed kittens, which underscore the immense appeal that kittens have in our daily lives.

*When one thinks of cats in connection with Edgar Allan Poe one immediately remembers his story 'The Black Cat.' But some prefer to think of the big cat who used to lie on the bed of his young wife, Virginia, when she was dying. It was very cold. They didn't have enough blankets to keep her warm and no money to buy more coverings. It seemed as if the cat knew this, lying close to her feet, trying to keep her warm.

At one modern publishing house, the resident cat lies on a pillow next to the computers, keeping the editorial staff company as they work. Even the designers encourage Sesame to sit with them as they work. She only occasionally runs across a keyboard or sleeps on the printer. When deadlines are looming and tempers flare, Sesame provides a little extra purr therapy, keeping the work flowing smoothly. She is an essential member of the staff.

Though cats, like many human beings, do not understand financial systems, there was one feline government employee who took a paw in the national budget with excellent results to himself. Philip Snowden, Britain's*

Below: *A British Shorthair with an obvious literary bent and a singular notion in the selection of subject matter.*
Opposite: *Another British Shorthair, at play amid a basket of dried flowers.*

Chancellor of the Exchequer in James Ramsay MacDonald's government in the early twentieth century, was said to be the most ruthless, icy, tight-fisted guardian of the state funds that ever ruled in the old Treasury Building in Whitehall. However, a cat named Rufus of England, but better known as Treasury Bill, wangled a pay raise of two cents a day in perpetuity out of Snowden.

Indeed, there had been a cat in the Treasury of England since the days of Cardinal Wolsey, Henry VIII's great chancellor, who, being a bachelor, made a great companion of his cat. But these cats have something more than social qualities. The rambling block of buildings at No 10 Downing Street, with paneled walls and shelves stacked with old papers, is a mecca for rats and mice. It was the job of Treasury Bill and his predecessors to keep the hordes down.

Bill was a noble ratter, but there came a time when his health declined. Sir Warren Fisher, Permanent Secretary of His Majesty's Treasury, noted that he was thin and languid. The matter came up at a meeting of departmental chiefs, and a minute went to the Lords of the Treasury, submitting that Bill's prewar pay of four cents a day was insufficient to provide a hunting cat with food now that the cost of living had gone up. An increase of at least fifty per cent was recommended.

Their lordships replied that after giving 'careful consideration to the case' they were 'unable to approve a raise.' Then Bill took charge. Finding Mr Snowden's door ajar he walked in and exercised some of those persuasions that cats know how to employ. The Chancellor looked at Bill and his hard gray eyes softened. He turned to his desk and made a note: 'Treasury vote: approve increase in cat's pay.'

Another well-known London cat was Mike, who was, from 1909 to 1929, one of the keepers of the gate at the British Museum. Black Jack, one of the old-timers, brought the kitten to the museum entrance in his mouth and left it there without any

Below: A pair of bicolor British Shorthair kittens. The variety of patterns among cats is as multifarious as the variety among snowflakes.

Opposite: Cats are not only appropriate pets for the house, but an increasing number of offices now have cats — providing there is enough paperwork to keep them busy.

explanations. Mike lasted, and became a great ratter. He was not paid in money but in good red meat.

Of course British official cats are not all males. Perhaps Emma Pankhurst saw to that, but at any rate female cats have played their part in official London. There was, for example, Emily of the Home Office, who was picked up in the street by a charwoman, but became so wise and engaging that she always sat in at conferences with the Home Secretary.

The United States Congress made a special appropriation for the maintenance of the feline guardians of Uncle Sam's mail. For nearly 20 years Champion Tom, the finest of them all, was stationed in the post office building at Washington, DC. Tom is dead now, after slaying so many rats that had they been laid in a row they would have stretched across the continent, or so it was said by his admirers.

There were cats in the Department of Agriculture as well, and during the

Depression the government paid a great compliment to their fastidiousness. A judge subpoenaed sixteen of them to sit in judgment on some relief beef, the recipients of which had complained that it was spoiled. When the cats ate it and meowed for more the authorities ruled that the meat was all right.

White House cats have also been well known. In 1993, after four years as home to a dog named Millie and her owners, George and Barbara Bush, the executive mansion took a turn to the feline with Socks, and his owners, Bill, Hillary and Chelsea Clinton.

One of the highest-paid cats known was Bobby, a self-made movie star in the 1930s, who died of old age at the home of his guardian, Charlotte Delaney, in Los Angeles. Bobby's mother was just a stray that Ms Delaney picked up on the street 15 years before. Bobby showed talent from his earliest kittenhood, and from the moment that he went on as an extra there was no doubt that he would succeed. He played opposite

Below: A pair of British Shorthair kittens who were born in the storage shed of a Pennsylvania antique shop and posed appropriately.
Opposite: A Himalayan posed next to a porcelain owl, which she vaguely resembles. While the cat is a generally graceful animal, this bottle of ink, if open, would be a prescription for trouble.

Gloria Swanson and many other stars while Ms Delaney watched and guarded his career. Bobby drew a good salary but he remained a simple, unassuming cat.

Another famous cat was named Morris. The large orange tabby was rescued from the pound in the nick of time, and his distinctive personality made him a natural choice for a career in television advertising that led him to receive star billing in the 1970s and 1980s.

Hollywood's movie studios have featured cats in a number of roles, from *The Three Lives of Thomasina* to *That Darn Cat* to *Alien*. Usually the cats featured in movies are American Shorthairs, the most common cat in the United States. In the popular television series from the 1990s, *Star Trek: The Next Generation*, the android Data has a American Shorthair named 'Cat,' who consistently refuses attempts by Data to train her.

Cats have always had a part in the traditions of the sea. The ancients identified the cat with the moon, the ruler of the tides. In

Below and opposite: In the past, distinctive pattern or color features of mixed breed cats, such as these, have been deemed desirable, and breeds have been developed to accentuate these features.

medieval times they had a sinister reputation, and in many parts of Europe, particularly in the highlands and islands of Scotland, people believed that tempests and disasters at sea were caused by cats — witches in disguise. But today, with no superstition about it, sailors value cats as good shipmates. They are not only useful in keeping down rats but in bringing good luck, often sensing and warning of approaching storms and other perils.

Cats do not like the water. Dogs do. Dogs are thrilled for adventure. Cats are supposed to love a snug, warm berth. Yet there is seldom a ship that doesn't have a cat. The annals of the sea are full of stories of them, while the only tales of sea dogs are the two-legged ones — the old salts to whom the name is colloquially given.

Cats have never said why so many of them hang around the waterfront, but certainly in seaports it is the part of the town they prefer. Perhaps it is because longshoremen and sailors are kind to them. Or it may be because of the rats. Or the moonlight on the water. Anyway, there they are and when one gets bored it takes passage on some ship and extends its knowledge of geography.

Dick, a black cat with white spats, made his home on the mezzanine floor of the French Line dock in New York and mingled with the crowd on sailing nights. He always took a voyage when he felt run down and returned quite restored by the sea air and tidbits in the ship's galley.

The steamship *Clairton*, plying between Liverpool, England, and Norfolk, Virginia, arrived in America one day with a Manx cat. He sailed as a stowaway, not showing himself until Liverpool was below the horizon. The people said the ship had never had such a smooth and speedy voyage and they gave

Below: The black coloring of this handsome bicolor tom fades to grey around his head.
Opposite: This kitten is oblivious to the inappropriate name he's been given, and as he grows up, the name will be far less important than the fact that his dish is kept filled.

the credit to Stumpy, as they named the Manx. Sailors believe that tailless cats are special carriers of good luck.

When the steamship *Leviathan* had left for Europe on her first voyage after being out of commission for a year, there was a rumor abroad in Hoboken, New Jersey, that she had sailed without a cat. A wireless was sent to the captain, Harry Manning, inquiring if this was true. He was so disturbed that he not only radioed back an emphatic denial but had himself photographed with a cat on each arm and mailed the picture to America. 'Was it likely,' he asked, 'that a boat that had twelve cats on its preceding voyage would sail without any?'

The *Leviathan* always did have fine cats. One of the old-timers was Ginger, a red cat born in a sampan in China. He was a grandson of Tiger, a huge tomcat who travelled with Captain Samuels of the clipper ship *Dreadnought*. Samuels would sooner have sailed without his first mate than without Tiger. At the last minute he would bellow, 'Is Tiger aboard?' and not until the people answered, 'Aye, aye, sir,' would he give the order to cast off.

Some sea cats have shown, on occasion, qualities of real heroism and devotion. The Coast Guardsmen at Cape Cod tell some stir-ring tales and some pathetic ones, such as that of the cat of the *Castagna*. After the vessel was wrecked she was found upon it, keeping solitary vigil by her dead captain's side.

Consider also the courage and intelligence of Old One-Eye and of Oldtimer, two cats of whom Captain George H Grant told in the *New York Herald Tribune Magazine*. On a night when his vessel was caught in a terrible hurricane Oldtimer made her way through the blinding rain and wind to Captain Grant. He was by the wheel house but she made him understand that he must follow her. Then she led him along slippery decks and down ladders to the after well deck, straight to where some heavy cargo had come loose from its lashings and was crashing dangerously against the bulwarks. It was Oldtimer's last service. On that same night she was swept away by a wave that broke over the boat deck while she clung there — on guard to the very end.

Old One-Eye, 'the most sagacious cat that ever trod the deck of a vessel,' was thought to have been born dumb. He meowed only twice in his entire life. The first time he woke the captain just in time. A drunken cook had crept in and was threatening him with a galley knife. The second time he

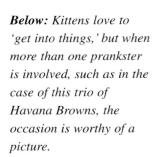

Below: Kittens love to 'get into things,' but when more than one prankster is involved, such as in the case of this trio of Havana Browns, the occasion is worthy of a picture.
Opposite: Nothing escapes the eye of the great hunter, poised atop his post adjacent to the berry patch.

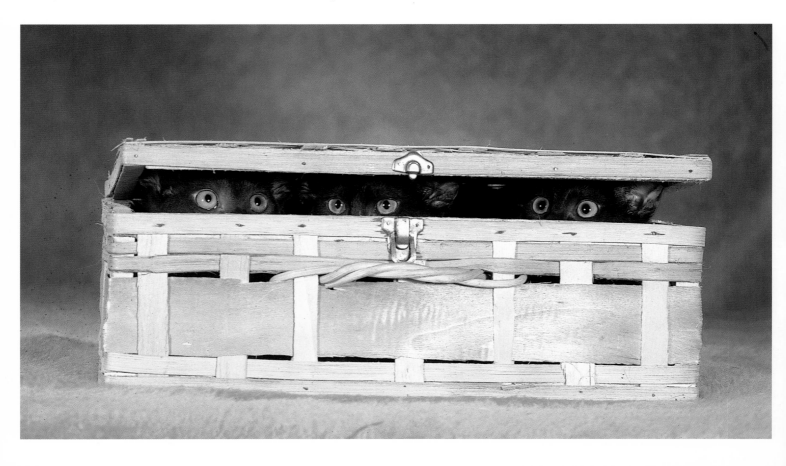

Below: One has heard of the amusing antics of the kitten on the keys, but when the kitten has a proclivity for brass in her choice of musical instruments, the results can be surprising.

warned of a drifting dory with two exhausted fishermen in it. It was a night so dark that they would never have been sighted. Did Old One-Eye see the dory or did he sense it out in the fog? The fishermen thought he might have smelt their fish but Captain Grant did not agree. He called it 'uncanny intuition.'

For many years the effigy of a ship's cat stood over the door of a house in Stockholm, Sweden. This house was recently torn down and the elderly recalled the deed for which this cat was honored. During a voyage from Haiti the captain and his wife both died. Their baby daughter was left with a nurse who did not know if the child had relatives or where to go to find out. The ship's cat, a former resident of Stockholm, knew where to go. As soon as the boat docked he led the nurse with the baby up one street and down

another until he reached 22 Vasterland Street. There he stopped and meowed at the door. It was the home of the baby's grandmother.

One hears a great deal about dogs on polar expeditions. In heavy work, like hauling sledges, they are more useful than cats could be. But even in the eternal snows cats have their uses. Lincoln Ellsworth took a cat along on the last Ellsworth Transantarctic Flight Expedition, and on Christmas night she presented him with three kittens. It was a pleasant little touch of home. Ellsworth sent announcements to the newspapers but no one knows why he didn't arrange to have the kittens go on the air. The barks of the Byrd Expedition dogs and the squawks of penguins were broadcast. Surely the meows of polar Christmas kittens were quite as worthy of the radio.

Below: A lovely, fluffy Himalayan at play in her owner's house plants. Cats like to nibble and one should take care that the house plants are not poisonous to their pets.

When Chappie the Globetrotter opened his eyes behind the counter in a little stationery shop in New York, his mother had no idea that he was to become a great traveller. She was a humble creature who had never been a block away from home, and Chappie was the smallest of her kittens. He was beautifully striped in black and grey and he had six toes on each foot, but he was frail and rickety. A few weeks later, a customer asked if she could have him. The shopkeeper said that she could.

The customer was Alice Engel, a cat lover who was going on a long trip through Europe and the Orient and wanted to take a cat as a travelling companion. The kitten's six-toed feet marked him for distinction, so she named him Chappie the Globetrotter and trained him for his job. Good food made him strong and healthy and daily walks on a leash taught him to regard strange sights and sounds with equanimity.

Ms Engel wrote the managers of the Italian Cruise Line and asked if she might take her cat in her cabin and the price of his

Below: *The real and the stylized, a black and white kitten posed with a 'Kit-Cat' clock.*
Opposite: *Nap time. A fluffy mixed breed kitten finds her favorite spot on the sofa.*

passage. They replied that they would be delighted to have him as a guest and inquired about his favorite foods.

Chappie had his own little suitcase which contained his dishes for food and water, scissors for cutting up his beef, his brush and comb, his bed, his litter box and some simple medicines. For cold days on deck he had a tweed coat and for mild weather a wool sweater. In his pocket he carried a bill of health from a New York veterinarian for the foreign quarantine authorities.

Chappie proved to be an excellent sailor. He was seasick only once, in a choppy sea off Gibraltar. But during a rough Atlantic crossing, when some racehorses aboard the ship nearly died of seasickness and 'Bring 'Em Back Alive' Buck was staying up nights with four unhappy baby elephants, Chappie sat for hours watching the waves through a porthole or from the deck. The higher they rose the more he enjoyed it.

Ms Engel's itinerary took her into southern Europe, Egypt, India, China, Japan and Hawaii. Railroad officials everywhere were polite to Chappie. He rode in her compartment, sitting up on the seat beside her like a little child, looking with interest at the sights that flashed past and the people in the stations. Sometimes he rode free and occasionally there was a small charge for his fare. Ms Engel kept him on a leash but it wasn't really necessary. He would sit quietly wherever she told him. It was only when the customs people approached his suitcase that he lost his splendid poise.

Chappie liked riding in anything except airplanes. He would not travel by air, so Ms Engel never flew. She and Chappie were too used to each another to be separated.

Chappie always kept his suitcase beside him, well plastered with foreign labels and ready for another journey. Ms Engel said they had only one bad experience during

Below: In search of prey that scuttles through the grass, this tom catches the sound of a promising quarry.
Opposite: A Domestic Shorthair with attractive tiger stripes.

their two year trip. A steamship captain refused to honor the written permission given to her with her ticket to take her cat to her cabin. He told her she must leave Chappie in the hold. She refused. She was put off on the dock with Chappie and their baggage. This was, unfortunately, an American ship.

European railways have always been more tolerant of cat travellers than American railroads, but today, regulations are strict everywhere. There is a story of a remarkable English cat named Mickey who has travelled thousands of rail miles with his people, Mr and Mrs Osborne Leonard, staying with them at every hotel. Mickey's family left him at home once and he cried so mournfully that they never left him again. He loves to take long walks with them, especially in

Below: This very young kitten imagines himself to be a great hunter. Perhaps when he grows up he will be. For the time being, he provides amusement for his owner. **Opposite:** *A little blue-eyed tiger caught in the act.*

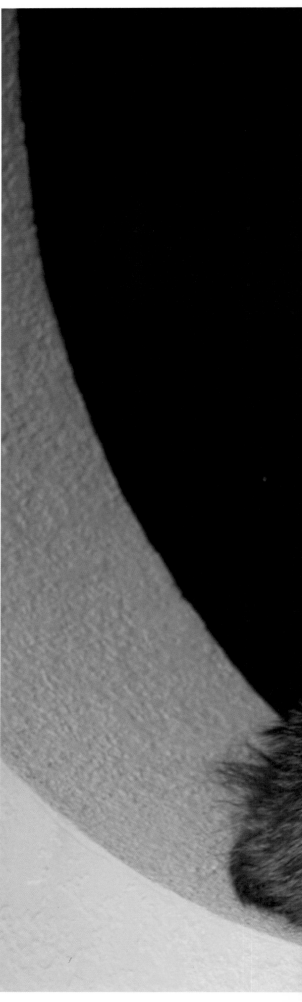

London and other big cities. He used to go out by himself, even in strange places, carefully smelling the doorstep so he could identify the building when he returned. The Leonards almost lost him on one such foray, but luckily he was rescued by a friend, so now he stays inside while the Leonards are on the road.

Recently, in the United States, a cat that was travelling in a cat carrier escaped into the baggage compartment of the airplane. She criss-crossed the country, while at every stop the baggage carriers and company officials attempted to lure her out. Food, water, nothing could make her emerge. After nine days of air travel and daily updates in every newspaper and television news broadcast in the country, she was finally rescued and returned to her happy family.

Many families in America travel by car, and their cats can be seen sleeping in back windows or amusing the toddlers on long trips. Maui, a large white Persian, travels with a harness and leash and will walk with his young owner, James, at rest areas. Maui is not fond of dogs however, so he must be watched carefully to avoid confrontations. Since he has no fear of falling, the windows are always rolled up, and if it is hot the family uses the air conditioner. He likes to sit on

Below: A longhaired cat enjoys the first sunny day of spring.
Opposite: Cat doors allow our pets the freedom and flexibility to come and go as they please. This appeals to the independent nature of cats.

Below: Nature's living gold: A kitten snuggles into a basket of flowers.
Opposite: This pair of pals demonstrates the tendency of cats to like to use one another as pillows even when actual pillows are present.
Overleaf: An engaging little house cat.

the seat or on James' lap and look out the window.

Fortunately for cats, in both the United States and the former Soviet Union, dogs and monkeys were decided to be appropriate experimental subjects in the first forays into space. Perhaps the cat's independent nature determined this. Or, in a more practical vein, researchers may not have relished the idea of attempting to remove a spitting, clawing cat from a space capsule.

SHORTHAIRED CATS

Below: The American, or Domestic, Shorthair is bred for a balanced conformation rather than for specifics of color or form.
Opposite: *A young American Shorthair prowls the garden.*

Today, although longhaired cats are extremely popular, the most common pet cat is a shorthair. People often say that 'He's just an an alley cat, but we love him,' but no one should apologize for their household cat because of the unfounded notion that its short hair implies inferiority or lack of a pedigree. Many breeds of cats were originally 'alley cats' in their native countries, and indeed shorthaired cats are the oldest recorded breeds.

Cats are believed to have migrated to Europe from Egypt, Asia and Africa by way of Gibraltar. From Europe, sailors probably carried cats to England. They may have mated with the wild cats native to the north of England, but shorthaired cats still largely resemble the ancient Kaffir cats of Egypt. Being great sailors, the invasion of America was only a question of time. In fact, domestic cats arrived on the *Mayflower* with the Pilgrims. Today, the various shorthaired breeds range from the American, or Domestic, Shorthair to the exotic Egyptian Mau and the nearly hairless Sphinx.

The shorthaired Abyssinian cat is believed by many experts to be the direct descendant of the sacred Egyptian cats. Many of the lit-

tle mummies found in Egypt resemble the modern Abyssinian's distinctive coloring. There were, however, also many blue and black cats in Egypt. Still, they may share the Kaffir cat as an ancestor. Other experts disagree. Professor HC Brooke believed that the Abyssinian is descended from the African Caracal lynx, which, like the yellow African Kaffir cat, will mate with domestic cats. This species of lynx can also be tamed if captured when very young. The Caracal lynx also shares the ruddy coat, tufted ears and general appearance of the Abyssinian.

One theory points to the coast of the Indian Ocean and parts of Southwest Asia as the original home of the Abyssinian. Indeed, Abyssinia — now Ethiopia — was located on the key trade routes where the Red Sea intersects with the Indian Ocean and the Horn of Africa. The earliest identifiable Aby is a taxidermal exhibit in the Leiden Zoological Museum in Holland. Purchased around 1835 from a supplier of small wild

Below and opposite: Two views of Abyssinians with their favorite toys. Abys have a smooth coat and graceful conformation. Breeders and owners consider proportion and general balance over size.

cat exhibits, the stuffed cat was labeled by the museum's founder as 'Patrie, domestica India.' On the other hand, some cat fanciers insist that the Abyssinian is merely the result of careful breeding of tabbies and that all other stories of their origins are merely legends.

The first published mention of an Abyssinian was in 1874. The book *Cats, Their Points, Etc* by Gordon Staples pictured a cat, named Zula, who was brought to England by Captain Barrett Lennard and his wife. An Abyssinian cat named Gondor is recorded in the first Cat Register, published in 1898. By 1905 there was a pair of Abyssinians registered in Boston.

The Abyssinian is a very active breed, not recommended for small apartments. Affectionate and playful, they are also great hunters of mice, birds and anything else that moves. They love to lie on tree branches, basking in the sun like the lions they resemble. They are often called 'Little

Lions' because of their coloring and wild appearance.

The families of Abyssinians report that they like dogs and children, will walk on a leash and can be taught to retrieve. They tend to bond with only one person in the family. The Abyssinian is the ideal cat for the man who thinks he hates cats.

Another ancient Egyptian breed is the Egyptian Mau. A wall painting from about 1400 BC shows a spotted cat on a hunting expedition, and a papyrus from 1100 BC pictures the sun god, Ra, in the form of a spotted cat. Despite the decline of the ancient Egyptians, their cats survived in the homes and the streets of Egypt. The Egyptian Mau is the only naturally spotted breed of cat. All other spotted breeds are man-made, specially bred to have the appearance of a wild cat.

All of today's Egyptian Maus are descended from the three cats that the exiled Princess Nathalie Troubetskoy brought to Italy in 1953. Her cats were first shown at the Empire Cat Show in London in 1957. These beautiful spotted cats with gooseberry green eyes have captivated cat lovers ever since.

Also descended from the ancient cats of Egypt are the common American Shorthairs, or the alley cats of the world. Among these

Below: An Egyptian Mau relaxes amid artifacts with which his ancestors would have been familiar. *Opposite:* A good overall view of an Abyssinian. The ideal cat of this breed will be lithe and muscular, although color is the most important breed characteristic.

Below: A beautiful white American Shorthair proudly admires his counterpart through the looking glass.
Opposite: The American Silver Tabby is a type of American Shorthair.

strays and hoboes, cats without benefit of breeding, living in holes and corners, there are breathtakingly beautiful kittens. It is interesting to see the pure whites, blacks and varied coloring and form among these so-called alley cats. Breeders have taken great pains to preserve the purity and beauty of their Persians, yet nature takes care of the shorthairs without any fuss.

The first American or Domestic Shorthairs were registered at the turn of the century, and they were imported from England. Today's breeders can trace the bloodline of their precious shorthairs for many generations, often all the way back to those few pioneers of the early 1900s.

It was traditionally said that domestic cats are 'the Cinderellas of their race,' sitting in chimney corners and doing the mouse-catch-

ing of the house. They are very practical pets. It is usually the common shorthaired cats who go down to the sea in ships and who patrol the farms and stores of the world for rats. They have an intelligence which has been sharpened through many generations by the necessity of scrambling for a living, but hardships have not marred their native courtesy. Once a cat's trust is gained, it will wind about the ankles, purring as if a long lost family member has been found. In fact, it will happily go home with its new-found friend.

Little Boy, a red tabby shorthair, moved from Hawaii to Arizona. His owner, Roberta Patrick, had started working for the Rainbow Acres Ranch for Mentally Retarded Adults. 'The young people in our house would come in and tell Little Boy all about their problems,' Roberta said. 'He always had lots of love for everyone. After nine years of 24-hour-a-day duty, Little Boy retired when I

moved into an office job.' Former house-mates still visit and ask about Little Boy.

Originally there were few Domestic Shorthairs exhibited in cat shows, but the owners of those cats, when asked where their stock came from, said 'Oh, just a couple of cats that I picked up.' A shorthaired silver tabby that began life as a stray recently took second best in the New York Cat Show. Although the Domestic Shorthaired cat is common throughout the world, each country seems to have its own special breed, unique from all the others.

The British Shorthair is a distinctively different breed from the American Shorthair. Although both cats had the same origins, the British breed has a uniquely 'square' look, with a short, sturdy body and dense fur. Like many other breeds, after Persians and Siamese were brought to England, the British Shorthair was largely ignored. The breed was nearly extinct by the end of World

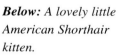

Below: *A lovely little American Shorthair kitten.*
Opposite: *A British Shorthair kitten. The tabby pattern is common on cats of this breed.*

War II, and breeders were forced to use Siamese and Persians in their breeding programs. It took many generations of work to bring the British Shorthair back to its original form.

Today, the British Blue, a distinct color variation on the British Shorthair, is one of the most popular breeds in the United Kingdom. However, blues were not always considered unique. Harrison Weir, the nineteenth century artist and author of *Our Cats and All About Them* who arranged the first cat show at the Crystal Palace in London, declared that the blues were just a variant of black cats. Indeed, the earlier blues had a dark streak along the spine, but breeders have worked hard to eliminate this characteristic and produce the true, even lavender blue which is the ideal today.

Similar to the British Blue, the Chartreux was created by the Carthusian monks in France. Famous for their Chartreux liqueur, the monks bred the blue cats as hunters of mice. The French poet du Bellay lauded the Chartreux as a formidable ratter as early as

1558, and by the eighteenth century the cat was recognized as a separate breed by the naturalists Linnaeus and de Buffon. The French novelist Collette wrote of her own cat, 'The sun played on her Chartreux coat, mauve and blue like a wood pigeon's neck.'

This breed requires space to move around, preferably a garden or large patio. The cat loves children and large dogs as long as it is treated with respect. Pet birds and rodents should be kept in sturdy, cat-proof cages since the hunter's instincts are still an important part of the Chartreux's nature. Decimated by World War II, the true Chartreux nearly became extinct in France, but is now making a comeback there, and in the United States, where the Chartreux has been enjoying much popularity since the 1970s.

The Russian Blue is believed to be descended from the blue cats, with thick, short fur, like plush, that were first brought to England from the White Sea port of Archangel by sailors. The double coat, like that of a seal or beaver, must have been a

Below: A stunning blue-grey Chartreux. This color, a breed standard, is an essential feature in breeding. Originally bred by Carthusian monks, Chartreux are one of the oldest breeds.
Opposite: *The classic British Shorthair is more compact than its American counterpart.*

Below and opposite: The Russian Blue is a distinctively fine-boned cat, whose blue coat is soft and dense.

desirable feature in the frigid weather of Russia. For a time, the Russian Blues were bred to an Oriental standard, but since the middle of the twentieth century, many breeders have brought the cat back to its original appearance. Anyone who sets out to raise Russian Blues can plan on having difficulty in trying to breed to standard. Besides the small litters and tendency toward white hairs in the coat, cats kept permanently in a warm climate begin to lose their double coat.

It has been said that the best cats are usually raised in a cold climate. An example would be Siegfried, a magnificent male

raised by Shirley Turner and Elsie Bunker on the Bunker farm in Merrick, Long Island. He was a brave cat, but very fatherly, not at all above tending baby kittens when their mother went gallivanting. Unlike many cats, Siegfried liked water and occasionally swam in the local pond, although he usually waited for hot weather.

While the European and British short-haired breeds are very popular, it is an Oriental cat which has caught the eye of thousands of cat fanciers around the world. A cat may look at a king, but not many cats have the opportunity to live like one. Siamese cats have, however, traditionally dwelt in the royal palaces at Bangkok in Thailand, which was traditionally known as Siam. Those who did not live at court lived in temples and had priests to serve them. They are not only royal but sacred, the modern prototype of the sacred cat of Egypt. The origin of the breed is obscure. They may have come from crosses between the sacred cats of Burma and the Annamite cats when the Siamese and the Annamese conquered the empire of the Khmers of Cambodia about three centuries ago.

The first Siamese cats to leave Thailand were possibly the two beautiful specimens that were given to an English woman by King Prajadhipok's uncle in the nineteenth century. They founded the line which soon became popular in England, and later in America. The first Siamese cat in the United States was probably the pet of First Lady Lucy Webb Hayes, the wife of President Rutherford B Hayes. He lived in the White House, a gift from David Stickles, the United States Ambassador to Bangkok.

Siamese cats are alert and appear to be interested in everything they see. It has been said that a Siamese cat is more energetic and can be in more places at once than any other member of the *Felis domesticus*. Devotees of the Siamese insist that they are the smartest cats in the world. However, every

Below: A Siamese kitten. *Opposite:* This adult Siamese demonstrates the classic breed characteristics, including the graceful, svelte body and the distinctive coloration.

cat-lover knows that his or her cat, be it Siamese or Persian or Manx or plain alley, is the smartest cat in the world.

The coat of the Siamese is soft, short and glossy. The body is a clear, pale fawn, the face is deep chocolate brown shading to fawn between the ears, and the ears, tail, legs and feet are brown. Siamese kittens are born snow white, but the distinctive markings soon appear, and at one year of age these cats attain a lovely contrast between fawn and brown. After this they slowly darken. The eyes of the Siamese are blue, and almond-shaped, with a slight slant toward the nose.

There is also a blue-point Siamese, in which the body is pale blue and the face, legs, and tail dark blue. The pigmentation of the blue point is a recessive trait. If a seal point is bred to a blue point the darker coloring of the former will prevail among the kittens.

The Korat, a cousin of the Siamese, is rare even in its native land of Thailand. Originally, these cats, first bred in the city of Korat, could be given only as gifts, and it was the custom to give a Korat to princes and dignitaries as a sign of devotion.

Thailand's King Rama V named the breed when he remarked, 'What a pretty cat. Where is it from?'

In *The Cat Book Poems*, they are listed as one of the 17 types of good luck cats. A Thai poet wrote about the Korat, 'whose hairs are smooth with roots like clouds and tips like silver' and 'whose eyes shine like dewdrops on a lotus leaf.'

The Korat, like the Siamese, enjoy being with their owners. They are good with children but will not tolerate other cats. In Thailand, they have a reputation for being street fighters and extremely aggressive.

The eyes of the Korat are unique. No other cat has such large, expressive eyes, oversized for the face, with such depth and intensity of emotion in their gaze. As a kitten, the Korat's eyes are blue, but as the cat matures, they change to a luminous green.

In 1896 a blue cat entered in the National Cat Club Show in the Siamese class was disqualified for being the wrong color. The owner protested that the cat was from Siam (now known as Thailand) and there were many more like it there. The first Korats, Nara and Darra, arrived in the United States in 1959.

Below: Noted for its distinctive voice, the Siamese is also bred for its form and coloration.
Opposite: The Korat, like the Siamese, originated in Thailand, but it is here that the similarity fades. The Korat is definitely a distinct breed.

Another popular Oriental cat is the Burmese. Dr Joseph Thompson, a US Navy psychiatrist, was so captivated by the little brown cats of Rangoon that he brought one home with him. Wong Mau was a happy cat in San Francisco, especially after Dr Thompson arranged to mate her with her closest cousin, a Siamese. From this pairing, and breeding back to Wong Mau, came both the Burmese and the Tonkinese. Nearly all Burmese in the United States can trace their ancestry back to little Wong Mau. Later, in the 1930s and 1940s, Dr Thompson and other breeders imported more of the polished mahogany-colored cats from Burma.

This elegant cat is pictured in *The Cat Book Poems* of 1350 AD. The short, dense and glossy brown coat is the marked feature of the Burmese. In the United States, the brown or sable coat is the only color accepted by the cat fancy organizations. All other color variations are called Malay cats and are registered separately. In Great Britain and other parts of the world, all the cats are called Burmese, regardless of color.

Owners of the Burmese will argue that they are the ideal cat, combining the best of the Siamese virtues with a softer voice and gentler manners.

The Singapura is the classic example of the former street or alley cat. In 1975, three of these 'drain cats' were adopted by Hal and Tommy Meadow and taken to the United States from Singapore. In 1980 another cat breeder found a Singapura at the Singapore SPCA and imported it. From these four cats, an entire breed has been founded.

Below: *A pair of classic Burmese, with their rounded heads and piercing eyes.*
Opposite: *The Singapura is known for its expressive eyes.*

There is a very long waiting list for Singapura kittens. They mature slowly, not leaving their box until they are at least five weeks old. Like many human mothers, the Singapura dotes upon her kittens and will nurse them until the next litter arrives. The wistful, waif-like expression of the Singapura, and its small size, has endeared it to cat lovers. It is a loving, playful charmer, involved in every part of family life.

Humanity has used cats in many ways to express and to personify forces of good and evil. The Egyptian worship of cats was based on the belief that they were a manifestation of the divine. The Celtic tribes of early Europe believed that the demonic powers which surrounded and threatened them appeared most often in the form of cats — specifically large, black tomcats. The belief that cats enshrine the spirits of the dead has cropped up in various primitive peoples, but it was the ancient Japanese who gave the idea its most interesting form.

First mentioned in a manuscript to the Empress over 1000 years ago, the Japanese Bobtail is a familiar figure in Japanese art. It is seen in ancient prints and paintings, with upraised paw to symbolize good fortune. In Japan, it was traditional that a cat is born with a black mark on its back — resembling a woman in a kimono — which was thought to contain the spirit of the owner's grandfather or great-aunt. Thus it is that the Japanese Bobtails are also known informally as 'kimono' cats.

Such a cat was sent to a temple to be kept from bad influences, and these kimono cats were never given away, or knowingly sent out of the country. However, early in the twentieth century one was stolen and carried to England. A servant smuggled the cat, a female, aboard an English ship. The captain wanted to return her to the priests of the temple but public indignation over the theft was so great that he was afraid to reveal that he had her. Thus it was that little Kimona sailed

Below and opposite:
Today a popular cat in the West, the Japanese Bobtail was once a closely-guarded treasure in its native land. They are a familiar figure in Japanese art.

for England, and went to live with a family in Putney, who, according to an account written by Dr Lilian Veley in *Cat Gossip*, respected her traditions and gave her a happy home. Kimona was uncannily human in many ways and definite in her likes and dislikes. She refused fish, vegetables and milk, eating nothing but raw meat.

In the United States, the Japanese Bobtail is descended from the first three cats sent home by an American cat lover, the late Elizabeth Freret. She adopted many of the mi-ke, or three-color, cats while living in Japan, and when she returned to America she brought another 38 with her. The ideal cat has a face shaped like an almost perfect equilateral triangle. Its unusual kinked and bobbed tail is only about 4 inches long, and the hair fans out like a pom-pom, resembling a bunny tail. Traditionally, kimono cats have coats of white, red and black, but they may also have bi-color coats. Originally, breeders thought that the kimono cat was an unusually colored Manx. When they attempted to breed the Manx to the kimono, however, they discovered their error.

There is a statue in Japan that was dedicated to cats, not the sacred kimono cats but the little cats that were sacrificed to make catgut for the samisen, a Japanese musical instrument. It stands in front of the great Buddhist temple to Nichiren in the Yamanashi Prefecture, and one of the figures has a cat's head. The samisen manufacturers had placed it there because they were afraid that the spirits of the slain animals might return to haunt them and injure the samisen business. Incense is still burned there and prayers said to appease and propitiate the cats, assuring them that the manufac-

turers regretted the necessity of making them into samisens.

There are always new breeds of cats, either intentionally bred or natural mutations, which are being developed by dedicated cat lovers. One mutation resulted in the Rex cats, two distinctly different genetic breeds, which are very similar in appearance. Both breeds have short, curly hair, big eyes and ears, and long, whip-like tails. They are ideal for many allergic cat lovers since they have finer coats and seem to shed very little.

The first known Rex cats were born in the eastern part of Germany in 1946, but a breeding program did not get underway until 1951, one year after the Cornish Rex was discovered. These two separate lines appear to be caused by the same spontaneous mutation. Kallibunker, the first Cornish Rex, was born of a shorthaired mother and an unknown father on a farm in Cornwall, England. The owner, Nina Ennismore, contacted an expert breeder, and following his

Right: A winsome little Japanese Bobtail kitten.
Opposite: In the Cornish Rex, breeders are more concerned about the short, silky texture of the coat than with color or pattern.

advice, managed to establish a line of Cornish Rex cats. Two of Kallibunker's descendants were imported into America in 1957.

In 1960, a curly-coated feral cat was discovered near Buckfastleigh, Devon. A stray that had been adopted by a local resident mated with the feral cat and produced Kirlee. Kirlee's owner contacted Kallibunker's and the two cats were bred. Only straight-haired kittens resulted. It was then that they realized that they needed two separate breeding programs for the Rex cats. They also decided to breed toward different body types, the Cornish toward a Siamese look and the Devon with a broader chest and straight back.

Below: This young Devon Rex displays the elfin appearance that is characteristic of the breed.
Opposite: The ideal Cornish Rex will have a relatively dense coat with a tight, uniform marcel wave.

In the early 1960s, three of the German Rex cats were sent to the United States. These cats were crossed with Cornish Rex and produced curly-coated kittens. The German line of Rex cats is called the 'Lammchen' line and was discovered by Dr Scheur-Karpin. The two breeds were recognized in 1967 in Britain and in 1979 in the United States.

The Rex cats are very inquisitive, with an affectionate, yet independent, nature. They are also very talkative, with a high-pitched voice. Rex kittens are tiny and look like mice when they are born. Some Rex are born hairless and are considered to be non-viable Rex or Sphynx cats.

The Sphynx is a very unusual cat. It is nearly hairless, with only a thin down over

Below and opposite: The Devon Rex appears fragile, but is actually quite a muscular breed. They are very active and they like to be with people.

Below: Cute as a button, this Scottish Fold kitten is easily more cuddly than any stuffed animal.
Opposite: Virtually hairless, the Sphynx is a loving breed with high metabolism that eats often, but never seems to gain weight.

most of its body. The modern Sphynx is considered to be a spontaneous mutation, since most Sphynx-to-Sphynx matings do not produce hairless kittens. However, a Sphynx bred to an American Shorthair will produce wiry, curly or occasionally hairless kittens.

Historically, there have been hairless cats. It is believed that the first hairless cats were born in South America and that the Aztecs raised them. The Mexican hairless, now extinct, was bred in Mexico until the late nineteenth century. There have been instances of hairless kittens in various breeds

in France, England and Canada, but it was an alert Canadian owner who officially started the breed in 1966. The 'Canadian Hairless,' or Sphynx, are still quite rare, but are sometimes seen at cat shows. Cat fanciers are attempting to establish breeding programs to propagate the Sphynx.

The Scottish Fold is an interesting addition to the cat world. The breed is distinguished by its small, folded ears, large, round eyes and wistful expression. It looks like a ceramic figurine or a child's stuffed toy. A cat matching this description was brought to England from China in the 1880s

and caused quite a commotion. Up until that time, all known breeds of cats had upright ears.

The modern breed began on a farm in Perthshire, Scotland, in 1961 when William Ross noticed that one of the kittens had folded ears. Mr Ross watched over Susie, and when she produced two floppy eared kittens, he adopted one, Snooks. Mr Ross then began a breeding program. The folded ears are produced by an incomplete dominant gene, a spontaneous mutation. The gene is also linked to a deformity of the limbs, so British Shorthairs and American Shorthairs have been introduced into the gene pool. At birth, all the kittens' ears look alike. The folded ears become visible at about four weeks. These sweet-natured cats are natural hunters, as their ancestors were, but are content living indoors.

Yet another breed begun by spontaneous mutation is the American Curl. This breed is distinguished by its distinctively curled ears. All American Curl cats are descended from Shulamith, the original cat born in Southern California.

The American Wirehair is descended from Council Rock Farm Adams of Hi-Fi. He was born in an American Shorthair litter in 1966 and was the only survivor of a weasel attack. Adopted by Joan O'Shea, Adam is the forefather of the new breed. With the assistance of Mr and Mrs William Beck, Ms O'Shea began a breeding program. The Wirehair is still a breed in progress, with American Wirehair to American Shorthair and Wirehair to Wirehair crossings producing the desired tightly curled, thick, coarse coats. The kittens look like little lambs. Some kittens born with straight hair develop the curly coats later.

While a spontaneous mutation is responsible for some new breeds, others have been developed by breeders. They cross different breeds in search of a particular characteristic, such as color or personality. In the case of the Exotic Shorthair, breeders were attempting to 'improve' the American

Below and opposite: The Scottish Fold is known for its forward-folded ears, the most important of its breed characteristics, although the kittens are actually born with straight ears.

Shorthair by crossing it with the Persian. Because these beautiful hybrids were winning the prizes at cat shows, there was dissatisfaction among the fanciers of the true American Shorthair.

Jane Martinke put an end to this by creating a separate class for the Persian-American Shorthair hybrid. Essentially, the standard was written for a shorthaired Persian. The Exotic Shorthair is said to be for 'Persian lovers who don't want to be bothered by the long hair.' By crossing Persians with American Shorthairs, breeders have developed a cat with a dense, plush coat, small ears and a short nose. Originally Burmese and British Shorthairs were also used in the breeding program, but this is no longer allowed. The Exotic Shorthair is the only hybrid cross recognized as a breed. The cat must have two Exotic Shorthair, or one

Persian and one American Shorthair, or one Persian and one Exotic Shorthair parent to be registered. This good-natured cat is another ideal choice for apartment life.

The all-brown cat has been revered for centuries. The poets of ancient Thailand celebrated their beauty, and they were supposed to protect their owners from all evil. In the early 1950s, British breeders crossed a seal point Siamese with the brown gene with a shorthaired black cat, producing the warm brown sienna kitten, the first of what would become the Havana Brown.

Havana kittens look like bats, with their large ears and pink noses. Out of the box and exploring the entire house by the time they are three weeks old, these cats have unforgettable personalities, investigating strange objects with their paws instead of smelling them like other breeds. They will

Below: The Exotic Shorthair was developed by crossing the American Shorthair and the Persian. The result is a slightly long-haired shorthair that is often referred to as being a 'plush' cat.
Opposite: The Havana Browns are solid brown from birth, but become darker as they grow older.

happily perch on their owners' shoulders and raise a paw to greet people. Havana Browns love to play. Among their favorite toys are cardboard boxes, paper bags and computer paper dangling over the edge of the table. They enjoy the company of other cats and are happy living in apartments.

Essentially a solid colored Siamese, the Oriental Shorthair is an example of a breed created for cat fanciers. While historically there were solid colored cats in Thailand, this breed was produced by crossing white American Shorthairs with Siamese. In 1965 the manager of a cat show in York remarked, 'The BBC television paid us a visit and viewers were able to see us all in action. There was special interest in Ms Turner's experimental "white Siamese."'

Breeders are always finding new color combinations in breeding, and many of the Oriental Shorthairs came from other breeding programs. For example,

in the work in producing the Havana Brown, a number of lilac point Siamese were used. Some of the kittens were a solid lilac Siamese type and are also called Oriental Shorthairs. In some countries, like Britain, each color is known as a separate breed and collectively as Foreign Short-

Below: A pair of young Havana Browns. They are an eager and inquisitive breed.

Opposite: The Oriental Shorthair, while thin and willowy, is also an agile and well-muscled breed.

hairs. In the United States, they are all called Oriental Shorthairs. Like the Siamese cat, the Oriental Shorthair demands attention and is talkative, agile, intelligent, independent and inquisitive. They are not recommended for anyone who requires a tranquil environment. They enjoy perching in high places, like the top of the refrigerator, and the kittens like to refine their climbing skills on the furniture and curtains.

The Tonkinese is another hybrid cross, between the Burmese and Siamese. The coloring is softer, the points blending into the

body color, which is between the sable and beige of the two parent breeds. From the 1950s through the early 1970s, breeders worked at developing the Tonkinese. The breed was first recognized in 1974 in Canada. Like their ancestors, the Siamese, Tonkinese are cats with personality plus. They are aerial artists and especially like climbing and jumping, preferably onto a moving target, like their owners. They shouldn't be trusted around bird cages. They make wonderful pets, getting along well with children, dogs and other cats.

When cat breeder Nikki Horner heard the phrase,'I'd love to own a panther,' it piqued her imagination and she set out to produce a mini-panther for fans of the wild cat. In 1958, Ms Horner began by crossing Burmese and American Shorthairs. Although her first efforts were not successful, she eventually found a black American Short-

hair with eyes so copper that it was assumed that there may have been a Persian somewhere in its ancestry. By crossing it with a Grand Champion sable Burmese, she finally found her mini-panthers. Known as the Bombay cat, this breed has the look of a wild animal. This glossy, black cat with copper-

Below and right: An all-black breed, the Bombay was originally a hybrid cross between the Burmese and the American Shorthair which was developed for people who would like to own a panther without having the bother of the full-size jungle cat.
Opposite: The Tonkinese reflects its Siamese and Burmese breeding heritage.

colored eyes is well suited for apartment life. It prefers quiet, serene surroundings and likes to lounge with its owner. They are the perfect choice for animal lovers who might otherwise want a panther, monkey or dog.

Ivory colored with golden spots, the Ocicat was created by breeder Virginia Daly, who crossed a chocolate point Siamese with an Abyssinian. Her daughter named the breed Ocicat because of its resemblance to the ocelot. Since she was really trying to breed an Aby-point Siamese, Ms Daly had her cat neutered and sold him as a pet. When a Detroit newspaper publicized the beautiful kitten and the noted geneticist, Clyde Keeler, expressed an interest in its wild appearance, breeders began to produce more Ocicats. By using three breeds, the Siamese, Abyssinian and American Shorthair, breeders have succeeded in developing a gentle cat with a wild appearance. Recognized in the 1960s, the breed has been compared to the ancient Egyptian fishing cats and the Egyptian Mau. The Ocicat is one answer to the demand for exotic cats. Rather than remove more of the rare wild cats from

Below: An engaging group of Bengal kittens.
Opposite: The Ocicat is a large, athletic animal which is bred specifically for the pattern of its coat, which is seen as resembling the wild cat.
Overleaf: A pair of young Ocicats, different in color, but alike in pattern.

their habitat, the cat lover can have the best of both worlds — a 'wild' cat with a personality suitable for the home. For some, however, even the Ocicat and the Bombay are not wild enough to suit their fancy.

Wild species of cats are not meant to be house pets and cannot be domesticated. When imported and kept in private homes, they often end up in zoos or are destroyed. Therefore, breeders set out to develop an appropriate cat for the lovers of the exotic. The Bengal is such a new breed of cat, a spotted breed developed to suit those cat fanciers who really wanted a wild animal. The domestic cat was crossed with the wild Asian Leopard Cat, and after careful breeding, the gentler nature of the domestic cat has finally prevailed, although the appearance of the Bengal is that of a wild animal. The name Bengal was taken from the Latin name of the Asian Leopard Cat, *Felis bengalensis*. However, since Bengal is also the name of the striped Bengal tiger, breeders are discussing changing the name of the breed to Leopardette.

THE MANX

Manx cats appear to be very satisfied with themselves despite their having no tails, and one could almost imagine them saying to tailed cats, 'Why have a tail? You cannot catch mice with it, or fight with it, or wash your face with it. Its only function is to serve as a handle for naughty children to pull or, if you are a mother, something for your kittens to play with just when you want to take a nap.'

As to the value of a tail as an ornament, that of course rests in the eye of the beholder. People who own and admire Manx cats think that a tail makes a cat look awkward, and that the animals of their chosen breed are much trimmer and more graceful than the finest 'tail-wavers,' as Manx owners call cats with tails. Manx cats will not, as a rule, associate with tailed cats, but with their own kind they are quite friendly. As companions for human beings they are, their admirers say, better than any dog.

The 'mystery of the ships and the magic of the sea' envelop the beginnings of Manx cats, whose origin is associated with the Isle of Man. Legend has it that they came to the Isle of Man by shipwreck, leaving their tails behind them, if they ever had any. As the story goes, in the early nineteenth century, a ship was wrecked on Jurby Point, and 'a rumpy cat swam ashore.'

Before it was understood that the absence of tails in the Manx was due to a dominant tailless gene — known as a Manx gene — there were many attempts to explain why the Manx has no tail. Most of them were colorful legends. One stated that Samson used to swim the Irish Sea for exercise. He was passing the Isle of Man when a cat caught him and he nearly drowned. Samson cut off the cat's tail in self-defense and it has never had one since. There is also a story that the Manx cat was the last of all the animals to board the Ark, and so Noah, impatient to get underway, slammed the door on its tail.

There is also a tradition that there were tailless cats aboard the Spanish Armada and that two of them, escaping from a wrecked

Right: An all-white Manx. Note the long hind legs and the characteristic lack of a tail.
Opposite: A blue-grey Manx kitten at play with friends across the mirror and off-camera. The Manx may be found in a variety of colors.

vessel on Spanish Head near Port Erin, were the ancestors of the Manx on the Isle of Man. Another story has it that the Adam and Eve of Manx cats were the survivors of a Baltic ship that went down off the coast of the Isle of Man. But no matter where they had come from, they became identified with the quaint little island in the Irish Sea, a feature in its trade with tourists and a part of its folklore. At the Jubilee Congress of the Folklore Society in London, in 1928, Mona Douglas discussed animals in Manx lore. She said that the Manx peasantry believed that the cats had a king of their own, a wily beast that pretended to be a demure house cat in the daytime, but at night travelled about wreaking vengeance on persons who were cruel to cats. They also believed that the fairies were friendly to cats and that it was of no use to shut the cat in or out of the house at night, for the wee people would hasten to its assistance and work their magic on doors and windows to gratify its will.

Naturally, with ships plying between the Isle of Man and England, tailless cats soon became common in Liverpool and other coast towns. They have never been as wildly popular as Persians or Siamese, and people who breed them do it not so much for commercial reasons as for the love of them.

The late Helen Hill Shaw, the secretary of the British Manx Cat Club, bred tailless cats for 40 years at her home in Surrey and she did more than anyone else to keep the strain pure. It was not easy. 'I never know what to expect in a litter,' she wrote. 'Even when two pure Manx cats are mated, there will almost always be one or two kittens with stumps or even tails.'

The cats in the Shaw home in Surrey lived together in the greatest amity. They slept cuddled up together, any number of them, of different generations and never quarreled. 'Home would not be home to us,' their mistress said,

'without the warm welcome of our little Manx family, headed by Champion Josephus, the latest of a long line of champions descended from the kittens I brought to England, 40 years ago, from a girlhood visit to the Isle of Man.'

Manx cats are very individualistic, very brave and active, and loyal and affectionate. Ms Shaw said that she once witnessed the reunion of a Manx cat and his mistress, from whom he had been parted for four years. 'He recognized her at once, jumping on her knee and then on her shoulder and kissing her, and he made it very clear that if he could help it he would not be parted from her again.'

The absence of a tail is not the only distinguishing mark of a Manx. The standard of points set up by the British Manx Cat Club says that a very short back and very high hindquarters are essential, since 'only with them do we get the true rabbity or hopping gait.' The flanks must be deep, and the rump round, 'as round as an orange.' The coat is double, very soft and open like a rabbit's, with a soft, thick undercoat of fur. Manx cats are found in every color, but color is not as important as form.

The absence of a tail is absolutely essential in the Manx. Although loved by their owners, many Manx cats would be disqualified in a professional show. In the show quality Manx there is a slight hollow where

Right: A small, bicolor Manx kitten. A small rise of bone and fur at the base of the spine is permissable in the Manx, so long as it does not stop the judge's hand.

Opposite: *While color of coat and eyes may vary between cats — or even in the same cat — the characteristic of taillessness is essential. The conformation of the head and body are also important.*

the tail starts in other cats. A tuft of hair is not a disqualification, but the hair must not conceal a stump, for a tail is no less a tail for being hidden.

The Manx cat arrived in America in the early nineteenth century. In 1820 the Hurley family owned a large farm near Toms River, New Jersey. The love of the sea was in their blood, and as the children grew up they owned their own ships, travelling far and wide. Among the curiosities they brought back were tailless cats. On the Hurley farm the breed grew and flourished and, when a son or daughter married or moved away, a pair of Manx cats went along. Farmer Hurley's descendants and the descendants of

his tailless cats have come down through the years together. Among them is Elsie Walgrove, his great-great-granddaughter, who breeds cats of this strain at her home in suburban Philadelphia. Her Manx are 'great hunters, not afraid to go far and wide from home, and very sturdy, some of the neuters weighing as much as 30 pounds.'

Perhaps some of the Hurley cats wandered away from the farm, because there were traditionally many tailless and bobtail cats around Barnegat, New Jersey, not far from Toms River. They were wild creatures, living by their wits in the dunes and dining on the leftovers of the fishermen's catches.

Below: A pair of Manx kittens, a bicolor and an all-blue.

The Manx cat is an indomitable character and Michael is a classic example. Michael is a handsome, coal-black giant of a cat, swaggering about on his tall hind legs and ruling the cats of the neighborhood with appropriate authority. He was one of the first kittens born to a petite Manx called Lena, and the only one marked with a tuft of hair. His owner gave the perfect kittens to friends and kept Michael because of his character. He is afraid of nothing and can find his way anywhere. Once he was accidently locked in the trunk of a car and taken to the other side of town. He came home all by himself, through many miles of traffic.

There is an old rhyme in which the Manx cat was the last of all the animals to board the Ark, and so Noah, impatient to set sail, slammed the door on its tail.

Said the cat, and he was Manx,
'Oh, Captain Noah, wait!
I'll catch the mice to give you thanks,
And pay for being late.'
So the cat got in, but oh,
His tail was a bit too slow.

Another version holds Noah's dog responsible.

Noah, sailing o'er the seas,
Ran fast aground on Ararat.
His dog then made a spring and took
The tail from off a pretty cat.
Puss through the window quick did fly,
And bravely through the waters swam,
Nor ever stopp'd till high and dry
She landed on the Isle of Man.

Thus tailless Puss earn'd Noah's thanks,
And ever after was call'd Manx.

Right: *The Manx is found in all the standard cat colors, including calico, as seen here. In addition to its taillessness, the Manx is also characteristically robust and rounded in appearance. The place of origin of the Manx is known, but not the circumstances, and this has given rise to the colorful legends and stories, such as the one told above.*

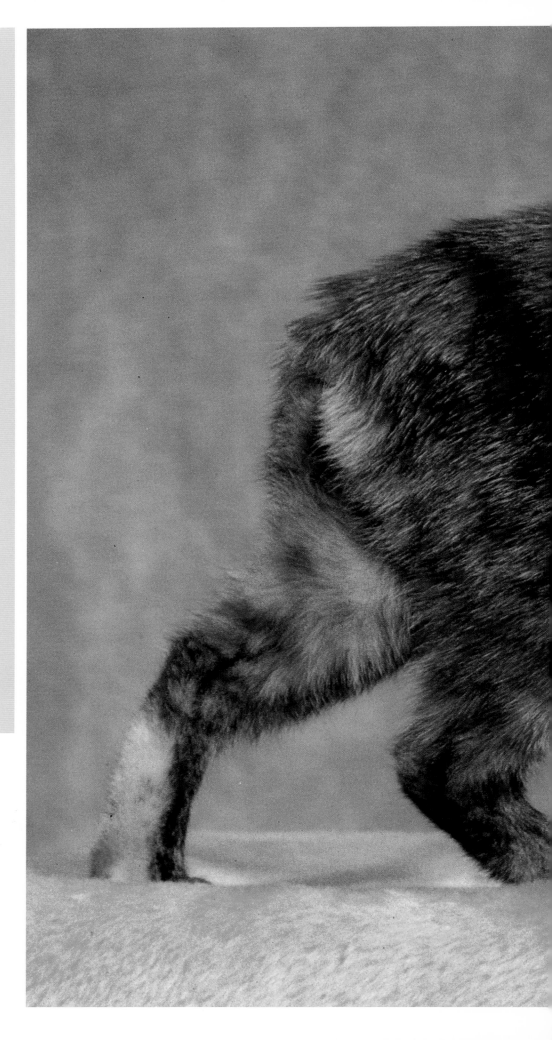

THE PERSIANS AND HIMALAYANS

Below: A small, grey Persian kitten.
Opposite: A white Persian in all her regal splendor.

One of the earliest recognized long-haired breeds was the Persian. Although the Persian was named for its supposed country of origin, no one really knows where they came from. The earliest references date from 1684 BC, in hieroglyphics. It is believed — albeit with romantic flair — that the Persian cat was brought to the west in the desert caravans from Persia and Iran, perhaps secreted in the baskets with precious jewels and spices.

While Persian cats came to Europe by way of Turkish ports such as Izmir, Angora cats originated in the mountainous region of Turkey traditionally known as Angora (Ankara). The Persians had silky, uniformly long and abundant coats and broad heads, while the Angoras had narrow heads and their hair was longest on the stomach, like that of the goats of their native country.

During the Victorian era and the early twentieth century, the Persian cat flourished

in England and Scotland. Scientific breeders like the Champion family, Elsie G Hydon and Evelyn Langston also produced Persian blues, chinchillas, silvers, tabbies and other varieties of the longhaired cat. The story of the experiments in pigmentation, of controlled matings which developed the many colors and shades of Persians, is far too long to be told here. Some breeders migrated to the United States with their cats, and then Americans began breeding Persians.

It was once a common misconception that Persians are delicate, lazy and not good mousers, but this is not true. One winter day in New York, Robert Claiborne picked up a bedraggled, emaciated cat on Third Avenue and took him home. He was almost at the last gasp, but with proper food and attention, he bloomed

Below: The Persian's round face and characteristic features are much more pronounced when she is a kitten.
Opposite: A classic Persian with his round face and luxurious coat.

into a handsome, urbane Persian, sinking gratefully into the lap of luxury. When Claiborne was transferred to the Far East, he took Black Pussy along. The cat passed quarantine and quickly took up his duties with his master's company. There were hundreds of huge rats in the warehouse. Black Pussy has cleared them out, and a sight it is to see him, with his tail like a plume, bringing down a rat almost as large as himself. He has also found other game. No lizard or crab is too much for him and once he killed a 10-inch centipede. He always brings his vanquished prey home as a gift for Bob.

The Himalayan is an intentionally-bred longhaired breed, a Persian type cat with Siamese coloring whose development took many years. A Swedish geneticist began the work in 1924, and two workers at Harvard Medical School continued the project in the 1930s. It took five years to produce Debutante, considered to be the first Himalayan. The Harvard workers were not interested in establishing a new breed so the torch was

Right: A pair of lovely, black Persian kittens.
Below: Two Himalayans in a basket. The Persians are distinguished from their Himalayan cousins in that the latter must always have blue eyes.
Opposite: A Himalayan kitten. Himmies, as they are known, come in a variety of colors, from seal to lilac, and from cream to chocolate brown.
Overleaf: A beautiful, classic portrait of a Himalayan in repose.

taken up by British enthusiasts. The British felt that Debutante was still too Siamese in form, so they continued with the breeding program.

Then in 1947, an acquaintance asked if they would accept her longhaired cat with Siamese coloring into the program. Her friend later wrote: 'When I saw this queen I was astonished at her beauty. Apart from her coloring she possessed no Siamese characteristics and was reasonably Persian in type.'

For the next eight years, this lovely cat was an important part of the British program. The British recognized the Colorpoint, or Himalayan, in 1955. Three years later a kitten won a prize for being the best longhaired kitten at the Kensington Kitten and Neuter Cat Club Show. In the meantime, in the United States, breeders were also working on the Himalayan. They presented their cats at a San Diego cat show in 1957, where the two cats dazzled both the judges and audience. Today, along with the Persian and Siamese, the Himalayan is one of the most popular breeds among cat lovers.

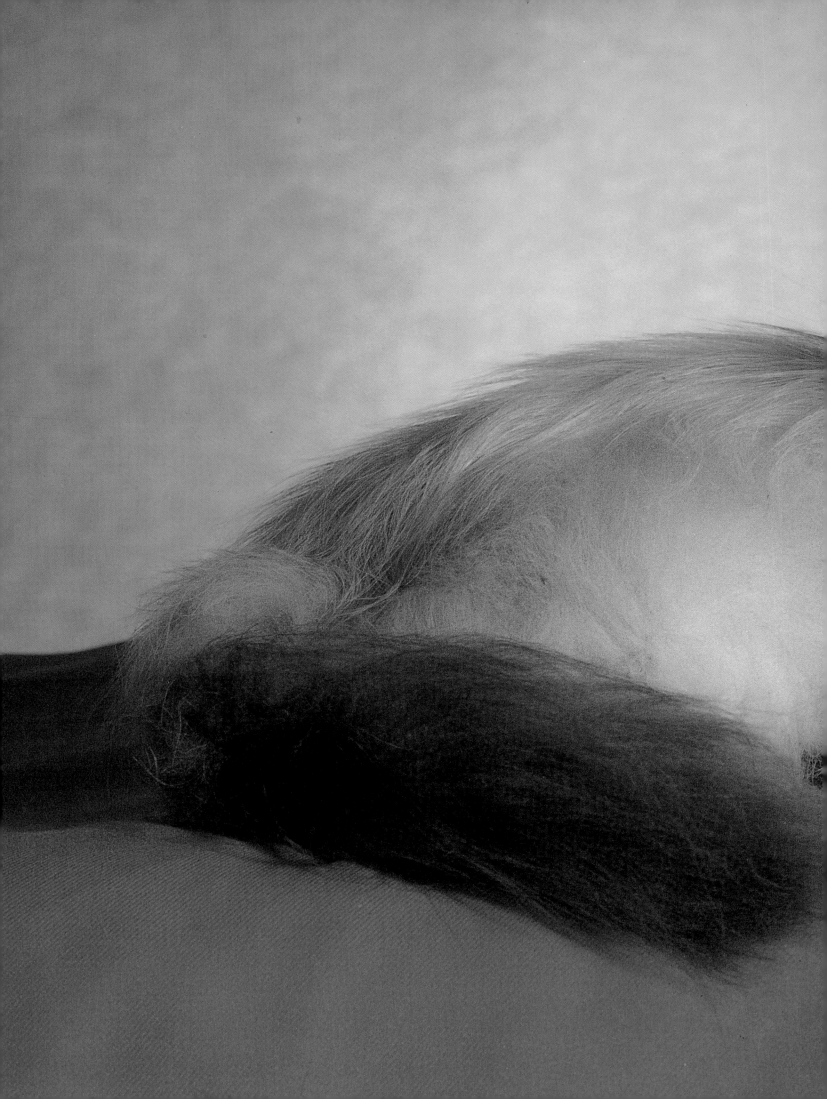

LONGHAIRED CATS

While the Persians have flourished, their longhaired counterpart, the Turkish Angora, was relatively rare until the 1960s. Since 1962, these cats have proliferated, thanks to a controlled breeding program at the Ankara Zoo in Turkey's capital.

Turkish Angora cats are believed to be descended from the Manul cat, domesticated by the Tartars and Chinese and which were known in the 1880s as Ankara cats. The Turkish Angora is a longhaired breed. Unlike the Persian, the hair is longest on the stomach, much like the goats of their native country. The head is wedge shaped, with large, tufted ears, almond shaped eyes and a rounded chin. Affectionate and playful, the Angora is the ideal cat for the active, yet sensitive, child.

Another Asian cat, the Turkish Van, is commonly believed to be a color variation of the Angora. Of course, when seen together, the differences between the breeds are obvious. The Turkish Van actually likes the water and is known in Turkey as 'The Swimming Cat.' The popular legend is that when Noah's ark reached its perch on top of Mt Ararat, the Van cats calmly swam out into the receding waters that became Lake Van. There they happily stayed. Historically, the first appearance of the Van was on the standard and shields of the Roman soldiers who occupied Armenia from 75 to 387 AD.

The first pair of Turkish Vans to be taken to England were gifts to Laura Lushington and Sonia Halliday, as rewards for work well done for the Turkish Tourist Board in the early twentieth century. Fortunately, despite pressure from other breeders who wanted to cross the Vans with other longhaired breeds, Ms Lushington proved as stubborn as her cats. After several trips to Turkey for more Van cats, the breed was truly established in England and recognized in 1969.

Turkish Vans love to swim. They are also notoriously stubborn. With their 'What, me worry?' attitude and affectionate nature, they are the perfect family cat. They tolerate children, dogs, noise and disruption with aplomb. The cat will help cook and steal only a few bites, crawl into the bathtub, carry clothing around the house like hunting trophies and keep its owner's feet warm at night. They are strikingly beautiful cats, white with auburn faces and tails.

Right: The beautiful Turkish Angora has a lithe, graceful body, a long tail and a luxurious coat.

Opposite: *The Turkish Angora probably originated in Turkey, and came to Europe by way of Italy and France in the sixteenth century.*

Another ancient longhaired breed, the Birman, is also called the Sacred Cat of Burma. According to legend, the spirits of the dead dwelt within the sacred cats, and these cats guarded the temples. One day, the Temple of Lao-Tsun — the temple dedicated to Tsun-Kyan-Kse, a golden goddess with blue eyes — was attacked. The head priest was killed, but his faithful companion, a pure white cat named Sinh, stood over his dead master and defied the invaders. As he did this, his fur turned to gold and his yellow eyes became sapphire blue. His face, ears, legs and tail became earth colored, while his paws remained white — a symbol of purity.

For seven days and seven nights, Sinh remained in front of the statue of the goddess, refusing food. Then, as the legend goes, he died, taking the priest's soul to heaven. When the remaining priests gathered to select a new head priest, the one hundred sacred cats of the temple paraded in and, to the amazement of all, the white cats had all changed to the same colors as Sinh. When they circled a young priest, it was taken as a sign from the goddess and he was selected as the new head priest.

The Birman was first described by a major in the British Army in 1898. While the exact circumstances of their

Below: An important breed characteristic of the Birman is that there is a sharp conttrast between the color of its overall coat and the color of its points.
Opposite: The Birman always has white gloves, with the rear ones often extending somewhat higher than those on the front paws.

importation out of Thailand is unknown, a pregnant female named Sita was brought to France in 1919. Her mate did not survive the long voyage, but Sita and her kittens established the breed and it was recognized in 1925. In the early 1940s they became well-known, having been shown in a number of European cat shows. Because of the extensive work of dedicated breeders they were finally recognized as a breed in Britain in 1966 and in the United States in 1967.

Today's Birmans are like the Siamese in color but have splendid, bushy tails and long hair. Unlike Siamese, they are a quiet natured breed, content to remain close to home and are ideal for apartment life.

The Balinese, or Javanese, breed is actually a recessive characteristic of certain Siamese bloodlines, and some Siamese litters produce longhaired kittens. Named for their graceful movements, much like the Balinese dancers, the cats have the same flowing lines and blue eyes as the Siamese. The coat is much finer, without a ruff, and the tail is like a plume. When breeders realized that breeding two of the longhaired

Siamese together produced longhaired kittens, the new breed was on its way. Like the Siamese, the cats love attention, but are quieter in voice and temperament.

One longhaired breed that definitely predates the Persian and Angora in Europe is the Norwegian Forest Cat. Records of this cat in Scandinavia go back into antiquity. These cats pulled the goddess Freyja's chariot in Norse mythology and are certainly the 'fairy cats' in fables written between 1837 and 1852. The ancestors of the Norwegian Forest Cat may have been a mix of short and longhaired cats brought to Scandinavia by traders and travellers. Because of the harsh winters of the Norwegian woodlands, the breed had to evolve to survive. Unlike most cats, in the winter the cats exhibit a unique double coat. The thick undercoat keeps the body warm, while the longer, oily outer coat resists rain and snow. In the summer the cat appears to be a shorthaired breed, except for the ear and toe tufts and tail. Fanciers began developing the Norwegian Forest Cat as a breed in the 1930s, and at least one cat was exhibited at a show in Oslo before World

Below and opposite: The Balinese was once referred to as the 'Long-haired Siamese' because of the obvious similarity in color and pattern. Actually, this name is literally acurate, as the the current breed was developed from spontaneous mutations in Siamese litters. They are now, however, named for the graceful dancers of the island of Bali.

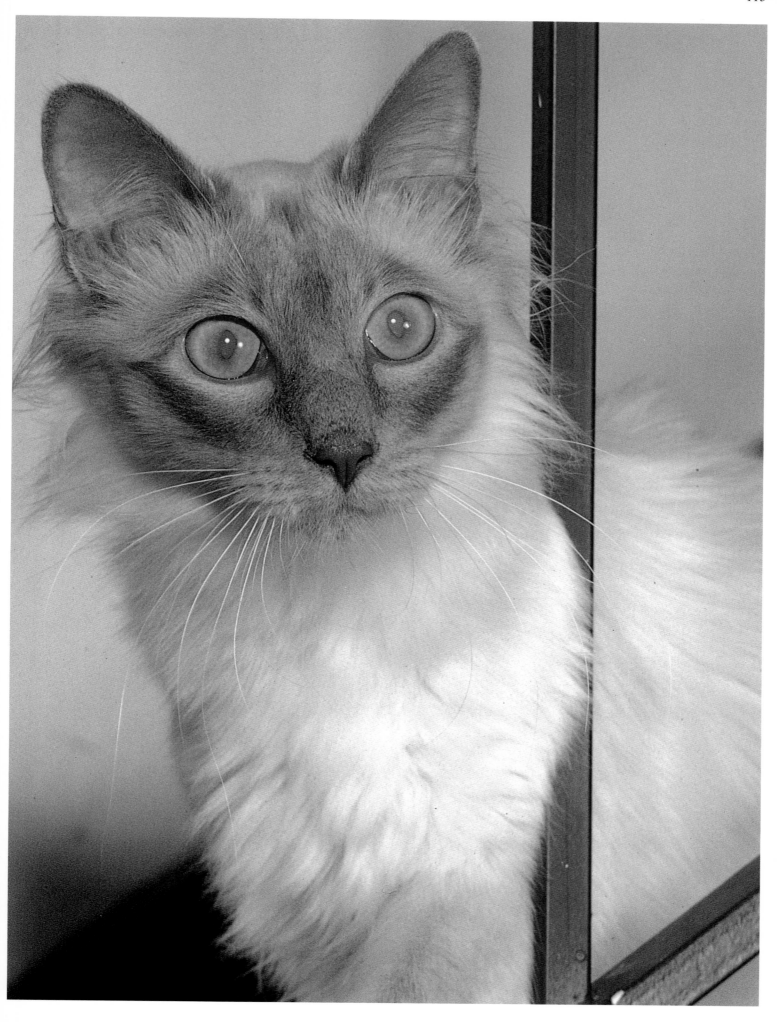

War II. Since the 1970s, interest in the breed has increased and the Norwegian Forest Cat was recognized in Europe in 1977.

The Norwegian Forest Cat is a newly popular breed in the United States, although there is a possibility that Lief Ericson may have accidently left one or two behind when he sailed for home from the New World in about 1000 AD. The captains and crews of the ships that sailed between the Orient and Atlantic ports may have also brought longhaired cats to America. In any case, longhaired cats have thrived in Maine, perhaps because of the cold climate, similar to that of their homeland. In Maine coast towns, a longhaired breed developed that came to be called the Maine Coon Cat. There is a legend that the Adam and Eve of the Maine Coon Cats were brought here by a certain Captain Coon and got the name from him. However, the generally accepted theory is that a Maine farmer saw an animal with a broad head and a bushy tail in his chickens and thought it was a raccoon. Then he saw it was a cat. It is easy to believe this story, since Maine Coon Cats can weigh up to 30 pounds!

These original cats were, like the American Shorthairs, house and barn cats, working cats. The breed fell into obscurity when Persians and Angoras became popular,

Below and right: Warm and cozy today, these kittens will grow into hard-working Maine Coon Cats. The breed was developed originally as a durable mouser that could thrive in the cold winters of Maine.

and it wasn't until breeders began to breed to a standard that the Maine Coon Cat received the respect that it deserved. Today, as the oldest breed of domestic cat in North America, the Maine Coon Cat is becoming more and more popular, not only in New England, but throughout the continent.

Dr Oscar, a Maine Coon mix, is the resident cat and the most popular member of the staff of the CARE Clinic physical therapy office in Grand Prairie, Texas. His staff position is called 'the tranquility therapist.' Many patients are surprised to see a cat when they arrive for their first appointment. Oscar is in charge of 'purr therapy' to

Below and opposite: The Maine Coon Cat was originally bred in Maine to hunt mice, not raccoons. The 'Coon' reference is to a passing resemblance that some members of the breed have to raccoons.

patients lying on their backs on hot packs. He is so enthusiastic about his job that sometimes he lies down on the hot packs before the patient. Massages are also supervised as closely as possible.

Oscar has had his share of close calls. For example, the night he was nearly shot by a policeman. The officer was checking the office building and saw something moving around in the dark. It was Oscar. Happily, the officer realized that Oscar was a staff member and didn't shoot.

Oscar is an essential member of the staff in more ways than one. Medicine can heal the body, but sometimes the therapy needed is more than just physical. Oscar provides the comforting patience that no human can ever give.

Several longhaired cats are the result of recessive genes in other shorthaired breeds. One of these is the Somali. Somalis are longhaired Abyssinians. When longhaired kittens began appearing in Abyssinian litters in the 1960s, breeders thought that some outcrossings had occurred. Later, they discovered that certain lines carried the recessive genes. While some breeders had their longhaired cats neutered, others found the long hair

Below and opposite:
Recognized as ideal 'people cats,' Somalis are friendly, adaptable and can actually be taught to fetch. Typically reddish in color, Somalis also occur in blue.

These pages: The
Cymric, a tailless breed
like the Manx, is consid-
ered to be purely a
descendant of Manx
anscestors, and not a
cross between Manx and
Persian. A relatively
recent breed, it was
developed thgrough
breeding Manx cats that
possessed a recessive
longhaired gene. A beau-
tiful cat, the Cymric has a
dense, luxurious coat.

attractive and decided to develop the new breed. The Somali was recognized in the United States in 1978.

Another such breed is the Tiffany, which is essentially a longhaired Burmese. It comes in sable with gold eyes, but since the 1980s, fewer and fewer longhaired sable kittens have been born in Burmese litters, so the Tiffany is one of the rarest of the domestic cats. Only one breeder in the United States is working with the breed. It will be many years before the Tiffany can be recognized by cat organizations as a separate breed.

The Cymric cat (pronounced *kim'rik*) is a longhaired Manx that was first discovered in Manx lit-

Below: An adult Ragdoll. The most docile of all cats, the Ragdoll is a very trusting animal and will relax completely when picked up.
Opposite: A Ragdoll kitten is the perfect pet for a gentle child.
Overleaf: A handsome Maine Coon Cat.

ters in Canada in the 1960s. It is the result of a recessive gene, like that of the Balinese, and mating two Cymrics results in all Cymric kittens. The Cymric has been called the most dog-like of cats, as it is loyal to one person, and can be taught to fetch.

The Ragdoll is one of the newest long-haired breeds. This plush cat, when picked up, relaxes completely and flops over, hence the name. The personality of the cat certainly also contributes to the appellation. The origins of the Ragdoll contain an urban legend, which tells that a Persian cat was struck by a car, and when her kittens were born they were unable to feel pain or fear, and refused to fight other animals. Though genetically impossible, this tale perfectly describes the placid, calm and noncombative Ragdoll, which must be carefully watched and is safe only indoors. Other animals and undisciplined children pose a severe hazard to these beautiful cats.

Index

Below: *An adorable kitten lounging on her owner's sofa.*